Cool Community Colleges

Creative Approaches to Economic Development

Stuart Rosenfeld

Community College Press®
A Division of the American Association of Community Colleges
Washington, DC

The American Association of Community Colleges (AACC) is the primary advocacy organization for the nation's community colleges. The association represents more than 1,100 two-year, associate degree-granting institutions and more than 11 million students. AACC promotes community colleges through six strategic action areas: national and international recognition and advocacy, learning and accountability, leadership development, economic and workforce development, connectedness across AACC membership, and international and intercultural education. Information about AACC and community colleges may be found at www.aacc.nche.edu.

Editor: Deanna D'Errico
Designer: Maxine Mills
Printer: Graphic Communications, Inc.
Cover photo: Welding students Angel Adam, Mary Kuebelbeck, and Stan Richardson at Bellingham Technical College in Washington prepare their entry for the "Junkyards War" welding rodeo. Photo courtesy of Bellingham Technical College.

Community College Press®
American Association of Community Colleges
One Dupont Circle, NW
Suite 410
Washington, DC 20036

Printed in the United States of America.

ISBN 0-87117-369-7

Contents

Foreword

"Make it new." Poet Ezra Pound gave that challenge to fellow poets several decades ago. He could just have easily been commanding an executive or engineer to "think outside the box" or "build a better mousetrap." Those are all ways of reminding ourselves of the power of ideas and of the necessity of cultivating the habit of originality.

I applaud the efforts going on in community colleges across the country, including in my own state of North Carolina, to marry Pound's mandate to their mission. In North Carolina, our community colleges are explicitly about the economy. Our mission is jobs—attracting good jobs with great futures, growing new jobs in new businesses, and teaching people skills they need to get and keep those jobs. That is why we were founded more than 40 years ago and why we are in business today.

Dallas Herring, the spiritual godfather of the North Carolina Community College System, said that the only valid philosophy for North Carolina is the philosophy of total education. That is particularly so now, with the tremendous need for job training and retraining occurring at a time when the study of the arts and humanities is often slighted. There has always been a creative tension between what we are and what we should be. How easy it would have been to

decide 40 years ago that we were either technical institutes providing only skills training or junior colleges devoted solely to academics.

Community college founders instead championed the Jeffersonian idea that the most important role of education in a democracy is to nurture citizens who are productive and responsible and capable of earning a living, making informed decisions, and stepping into leadership. How much does creativity count in that effort? It should count more than it ever has, because we simply cannot offer the same skills, in the same jobs, in the same industries as we did 40 years ago. Low-skill jobs for low-paid labor are gone to places where desperate people will work for even less.

A few years ago, a speaker at the Southern Growth Policies Board said that educators were focused too narrowly on boosting math and science scores. He cautioned that our competitive advantages in the world marketplace are the creativity of our workforce and worldwide admiration of our culture, and he called for increased attention to the humanities and the arts in the classroom. Community colleges must also recognize that the exercise of creativity is a legitimate way to make a living. Much of what defines a great place to live, work, and visit is its distinctive culture. We must support artists and thinkers in their work. We must teach arts and humanities across our curricula. We must sponsor exhibits, performances, and festivals as part of our role as conveners of public life.

In North Carolina, we have done some of these things very well. In Raleigh, we have for 9 years mounted an annual community college art exhibition. We usually have more than 120 pieces on display, prompting a wonderful addition to the workplace for colleagues and visitors. One of our outstanding successes was the Visiting Artist Program, a partnership with the North Carolina Arts Council that placed professional artists on our campuses.

From the 1970s until funding cuts shut down the program in 1995, hundreds of people came to our campuses as visiting artists. Many stayed with community colleges, creating arts programs where none had been before. Others built lasting arts institutions in their communities. Still others were already here, carving wood, telling stories, and playing music.

We also work to boost the skills of artists as entrepreneurs. A creative idea becomes an economic opportunity when it turns into a product that somebody wants to buy. One of my favorite success stories is the pottery program at Montgomery Community College. Pottery is a time-honored tradition in Montgomery and neighboring counties. In 1982, about 15 potteries were operating in that part of the state, almost all related to old-style pottery. Five years later, there were 50. Today, the area boasts more than 100 potteries and more than 300 people making their living in them. Montgomery Community

College's exceptional program is one of the most important reasons that Seagrove pottery has become an economic force. Program director Mike Ferree makes sure his students learn the craft of fashioning a sturdy, functional pot, the art of making it beautiful and distinctive, and the business of selling it.

Why do we have to ask whether support for the creative economy should be a priority in community colleges? Statistics show that creative endeavors drive tourism, attract prosperous travelers who spend lots of money, keep residents happy, and directly employ many people. Yet a significant number of people need convincing that jobs built on creativity are *real* jobs that people do when they grow up! This attitude seems to be built into us: Creativity is fun, so it cannot be real work. When economic survival depends on our ability to apply "making it new" to our industries, trivialization of creative endeavors makes no sense.

During my tenure as chair of the State Arts Council, I heard a wonderful story from Sara Hodgkins, who was then North Carolina's Secretary of Cultural Resources. Hodgkins, a musician by training, met composer Gian Carlo Menotti, founder of the Spoleto arts festivals in Italy and in Charleston, South Carolina. Menotti was holding forth about what he considered to be gaps in American appreciation of the arts. He said: "The trouble with Americans is that you think the arts are an after-dinner mint! No, no, no! The arts, they are the bread of life!" Indeed.

H. Martin Lancaster, President
North Carolina Community College System

Preface

Regional Technology Strategies (RTS) is a North Carolina-based nonprofit organization dedicated to developing and piloting policies and practices that create wealth for more people and places. In 2004, recognizing a new and more competitive environment for regional development with heavy losses of employment in traditional industries, RTS organized a conference to discuss ways that community colleges can and do support creative economies. The conference, which was held in November 2004 in Asheville, North Carolina, was planned collaboratively with the North Carolina Community College System, Hand-Made in America, and the University of North Carolina Office of Economic and Business Development. Planning of the conference was also assisted by the Trans-Atlantic Technology and Training Alliance (TA^3), an international consortium of leading community and technical colleges, which is co-managed by RTS for the United States and by CIRIUS, an arm of the Danish Ministry of Vocational Education, for Europe. The TA^3, whose goal is collaborative learning and innovation, meets regularly to collectively devise effective responses to new circumstances and emerging issues. RTS and HandMade in America organized the conference, which was attended by nearly 140 representatives of community colleges, economic development offices, arts councils, government agencies, industry, and the arts from the United States and abroad.

Asheville, a city of about 69,000 located in the heart of North Carolina's Appalachian Mountains, was chosen as the site in part because it has become known as an arts city and as one of America's most powerful magnets for all types of creative talent and enterprises. A 50-mile radius includes the well-known Penland School of Crafts, the John C. Campbell Folk School, Haywood Community College's crafts program, and surrounding towns with heavy concentrations of artistic creativity. According to an article in the Asheville *Citizen-Times,* "Asheville's cool factor is translating into a flourishing creative economy and cold, hard cash" (Davis, 2004).

The conference brought together experts and practitioners to share their experiences with one another and the audience and to develop policies and practices at community colleges that strengthen their local economies through more creative and innovative people and companies. It featured speakers—from Washington State to Massachusetts, from New Brunswick to Arkansas, and from Finland to South Africa —who are at the forefront of efforts to link arts and culture to economic development and quality of life. Presenters discussed ways in which they use art and culture to deliver programs, create businesses, market products, and produce more creative workers and entrepreneurs.

This book draws on the presentations and discussions from the conference to illustrate how community colleges can more effectively integrate the arts, design, and culture into programs and institutions in ways that build creative economies that contribute to economic development. It suggests actions for community colleges and presents a vision for the community college system of the 21st century. (For complete details of the conference and the original report, see www.rtsinc.org/asheville.)

REGIONAL TECHNOLOGY STRATEGIES, INC.

TRANS-ATLANTIC TECHNOLOGY *and* TRAINING ALLIANCE

Acknowledgments

This book is an adaptation of a previously published report, *The Art of Economic Development: Community Colleges for Creative Economies*, which documented the results of the November 2004 conference of the same name. RTS took the lead in organizing the conference, in collaboration with the following partner organizations whose invaluable support made the event possible and ensured its success:

HandMade in America, Asheville, NC

North Carolina Community College System, Raleigh

University of North Carolina, Office of Economic and Business Development, Chapel Hill

The following organizations provided support for the conference and the original report:

Appalachian Regional Commission, Washington, DC

Cherokee Preservation Fund, Cherokee, NC

Economic Research Service, U.S. Department of Agriculture, Washington, DC

Inn at the Biltmore House, Asheville, NC

Lumina Foundation for Education, Indianapolis, IN

North Carolina Department of Commerce/ Workforce Development Board, Raleigh

Progress Energy, Raleigh, NC

W. K. Kellogg Foundation, Battle Creek, MI

Winthrop Rockefeller Foundation, Little Rock, AR

I wish to thank my fellow speakers, moderators, and participants for the information they shared at the conference, which forms the basis for most of this book:

Rebecca Anderson, Executive Director, HandMade in America, Asheville, NC

Beate Becker, Founder and Executive Committee member, Creative Economy Council, Boston

Bill Bishop, Reporter, *Austin American-Statesman*, TX

Jon Brookhouse, Associate Professor, International School of Art and Design, Finlandia University, Hancock, MI

Jim Clinton, Executive Director, Southern Growth Policies Board, Research Triangle Park, NC

Marion Coy, Director, Galway-Mayo Institute of Technology, Galway, Ireland

Raymond R. Geary, Dean, Community and Economic Development, College of the Redwoods, Eureka, CA

Tim Glotzbach, Dean, Kentucky School of Craft, Hazard Community and Technical College, Knott County Branch, Hindman

Leoni Hall, Consultant, CreateSA, Johannesburg, South Africa

Judith Hansen, Past President, Independence Community College, KS

Heikki Jylhä-Vuorio, Dean, International School of Art and Design, Finlandia University, Hancock, MI

Robert Kavanagh, Principal, New Brunswick College of Craft and Design, Fredericton, Canada

Mary Powell Kirk, President, Montgomery Community College, Troy, NC

H. Martin Lancaster, President, North Carolina Community College System, Raleigh

Joanne MacInnes, Director of the Lily I. Juttila Center for Global Design and Business, Finlandia University, Hancock, MI

James F. McKenney, Vice President of Economic and International Development Programs, American Association of Community Colleges, Washington, DC

Mary Moe, Dean, Montana State University-Great Falls College of Technology

Nigel Paine, Head of People Development, British Broadcasting Corporation, London

Gerald Pumphrey, President, Bellingham Technical College, WA

Robert L. Pura, President, Greenfield Community College, MA

Greg F. Rutherford, Vice President, Economic and Workforce Development, Haywood Community College, Clyde, NC

Geoffrey Sutton, Director, Creative Enterprise Cluster, Helena, MT

Michael Tibbetts, Senior Manager, Creative Enterprise Cluster, Scottish Enterprise, Glasgow, United Kingdom

Patrick Tobin, Galway-Mayo Institute of Technology, Letterfrack, Ireland

Steven L. VanAusdle, President, Walla Walla Community College, WA

Jesse L. White, Jr., Director, Office of Economic and Business Development, University of North Carolina at Chapel Hill

Brad Williams, Director, Munro Foundation, Hot Springs, AR

❧

I would also like to thank Robert Donnan, who provided photographs for the original report and for this publication as well, and Cynthia Liston, Jana Shannon, and Daniel Broun, who contributed suggestions and edits to the original report.

1. The Avant-Garde of Community Colleges

Community colleges have become many things to many people over their century-long transformation from junior colleges to comprehensive learning environments. As relative latecomers to America's education system, they have been able and willing to take on missions and serve people that other education institutions could not or would not. Community colleges have become well known for their effectiveness in delivering education and training, supporting industrial development, and serving all segments of the population. Few think of community colleges as bastions of creativity or particularly cool places. Effective, yes, but not places with strong reputations for arts and culture, not places that are likely to attract students—or, for that matter, alumni, retirees, and knowledge-intensive companies.

Institutions of higher education such as the University of Michigan, University of Wisconsin, Bennington, Bryn Mawr, or Bowdoin offer not only strong programs of study but also environments where people prefer to spend their free time. Community colleges, in contrast, offer convenience and value to students and companies. Because so many of their students are local, have families, and work full time, they do not serve the same social function. Traditionally, people commute to community colleges—

sometimes from long distances—to acquire skills or credits or simply to pursue interests, and then they return to their homes, families, and jobs.

Yet many community colleges are unassumingly becoming places that students and communities do look to for leisure-time, creative, and cultural activities, and they are becoming institutions of choice for a growing number of people seeking education and training for creative occupations and industries. An increasing number of community colleges, particularly in small cities and rural areas, have large community or regional theaters and museums on campus; host artisan or writers' workshops, festivals, and concerts; and contribute to rebuilding main streets. They offer occupational and transfer programs in the arts, graphic design, architecture, crafts, film and video, animation, and other creative-class careers.

Community colleges, in fact, are becoming known as cool places. Wilkes Community College in rural North Carolina draws more than 70,000 people to its campus each April for MerleFest, a nationally known music festival that brings about $14 million into the area. Capital Community College in Hartford, Connecticut, by taking over a historic department store in the center of the city and retaining its art deco interior, has added immensely to the attraction of downtown. The Siler City (NC) campus of Central Carolina Community College operates the state's first arts business incubator and one of few in the nation. Santa Fe Community College's fine furniture program in New Mexico adds another dimension to the area's already huge visual arts and ceramics cluster. Okaloosa-Walton College in Florida

A student at the Kentucky School of Craft, Hazard Community and Technical College, uses technology to make an artistic bowl.

Photo courtesy of Kentucky School of Craft

claims the title of "cultural and artistic center for Northwest Florida" and is home to the Northwest Florida Symphony Orchestra.

Why have the contributions of community college to the arts, culture, and creativity—in the community, the economy, and workforce—received so little notice and respect to date? Perhaps it is because community colleges have been so successful in preparing the nation's workforce, so proficient in serving businesses, and so good at improving access to higher education that their civic and cultural contributions have been overlooked—and, unfortunately, sometimes neglected.

Community colleges have been renowned for supporting new and expanding industries, keeping the pipeline filled with new workers, and upgrading the skills of incumbent workers. They deliver an array of services, from industrial and information technologies to health and social services. Whereas universities are expected to anchor creative milieus and attract the most talented students with the highest SAT scores, community colleges are expected to support local industry, attract business investment, and educate residents of all ages, abilities, and persuasions in communities of all types. If community colleges have been successful with the niche they have carved out for themselves, why are they changing?

Crafting a New Strategy

Pressures on regions and community colleges to rethink and readjust their priorities are coming from unanticipated and unsettling changes in America's economic landscape and employment base. Much of the manufacturing base that covered much of non-metro America in the second half of the 20th century has now moved offshore to places able to produce quality products at lower cost. From 1990 to 2005, employment in the U.S. textile industry dropped more than 60%; in apparel, it fell more than 72%. Both industries are longtime staples of many rural economies (Federal Reserve Bank of Atlanta, 2005). A large share of those jobs has migrated to China, where one city alone, Chaozhou, now produces 510 million evening gowns annually; another, Datang, produces 9 billion pairs of socks each year (Barboza, 2004). The nation's smaller cities and towns now are struggling to find new jobs to offset the losses from abandoned factories and mills.

Although industrial attraction remains the favored economic strategy and represents the largest economic development expenditure in most regions and states, in competition among regions for new plant locations produces far fewer winners than there were in the latter half of the 20th century when, as one southern official remembers, about all a developer had to do to attract new investment was to face north and chant three times. The highest-tech and most research-intensive industries have been

Photo courtesy of Haywood Community College Professional Crafts.

Pottery student Robin Bryant practices her craft at Haywood Community College, North Carolina. Since 1974 Haywood has graduated and supported generations of successful business people.

Photo courtesy of EnergyXchange.

Mayland Community College, a partner in the EnergyXchange in western North Carolina, features a popular tourist attraction—a landfill that uses the methane released to power glass and ceramic studios and horticulture and aquaponics facilities.

clustering in particular cities that have both cultural amenities and strong research universities. Three quarters of the nation's highly sought-after biotechnology jobs, for instance, are concentrated in just nine cities (Cortright & Mayer, 2002). Regional economic developers in other places who understand these changes are finding it necessary to shift their tactics from offering incentives to recruit and hold onto industry to attracting and keeping creative people and investing in cultural resources (Rosenfeld, 2004a).

Sectors most likely to grow and create jobs are those with knowledge-intensive companies that employ highly talented and creative workers, those that have companies that depend on art and design, and those that produce artistic or designer goods or services. Firms most likely to succeed in threatened sectors in the United States are those that have advantages that are difficult to replicate—in the case of

furniture, for example, design, finishing, and marketing. Leading business magazines are beginning to recognize these advantages. "When people talked about innovation in the '90s they invariably meant technology. When people speak about innovation today, it is more likely to they mean design. Consumers, who are choking on choice, look at design as the new differentiator" (Nussbaum, 2005). The places that draw talented people and creative enterprises (and tourists) that can provide such advantages are proving to be cities and towns where there is a strong arts presence and a cultural and creative milieu.

Competitive advantages that result when art and design are embedded in products and services can induce customers to pay a premium for style. The success of Bang & Olufsen electronics or Alessi kitchen products in Europe—or Kohler fixtures, Lees Carpets, or Crenshaw

Student Jessi Knight works on a stained glass art window at Hocking College in Nelsonville, Ohio.

Lighting in the United States—proves that there is a market for fashion-oriented, styled products. Our industrial base has shifted from being able to compete through the 1970s by simply "making things cheaper" and "making things better" in response to Japanese and western European successes, to "making things more appealing" as Asian nations prove able to achieve high quality at lower costs. That strategy forces companies to rely more on innovation, image, and aesthetics (Rosenfeld, 2004a).

Moreover, consumer demand for authentic and unique goods, many made by small businesses and entrepreneurs, represents a growing proportion of many economies, particularly in rural communities. These small enterprises include a trade sector and attract tourism revenues. HandMade in America's research in western North Carolina showed that arts and crafts added $122 million in just one year to the region's economy. Perhaps the most compelling evidence of the economic value of arts and design is that they are starting to attract venture capital and grant funds. Art.com, a company (now in California) that already has 200 employees, recently raised $30 million to expand its Web-based art gallery and expedite an IPO (Cox, 2005). In 2005, the Commonwealth of Virginia awarded 10 of its 19 Appalachian Regional Commission economic development grants to projects to develop either arts and crafts or tourism based on cultural heritage. The most important aspect of these knowledge- and arts-intensive goods and services is that they are much more likely to be produced in industrialized countries that pay higher wages.

As more community colleges are realizing, embedding the arts and culture in the community, business, and social milieus can be a significant advantage for talented people and lead to the availability of high-quality jobs in the global marketplace, and it can provide the distinguishing features that give a place an identity that can drive economic development. If used to best advantage, expanding the arts and design in community colleges will

- *Give companies new competitive advantages.* This requires a new paradigm for education and training that goes beyond educating students to use new production technologies and techniques to educating students in the importance and application of art and design in product appearance, use, packaging, and marketing.

- *Add to community and cultural resources and amenities.* The community college, particularly in small cities and rural areas, is the institution with the most resources and greatest ability to amass the events and cultural venues in the community necessary to attract companies and tourists and retain young people.

- *Educate and support artisans.* Artisans collectively represent much larger proportions of some sectors of the economy than is commonly believed or that conventional data analyses reveal. They offer an underappreciated set of economic, employment, and entrepreneurial opportunities, even though they may collectively constitute a significant share of the economy.

- *Attract nontraditional learners with creative talent.* Young people with underdeveloped or unrefined artistic talents might be attracted into a community college by the right mix of programs in the arts, and once they experience success, they may seek further education.

- *Improve learning outcomes and students' labor market value.* A growing body of research shows that education in the arts can increase achievement scores in non-arts fields and also teach students ways to communicate creatively and express themselves—critical skills sought by employers (McCarthy, Ondaatje, Zakaras, & Brooks, 2004).

Kohler Co. in Wisconsin uses its Artists in Residence program and ongoing dialogue with the art community to inspire artistic creativity and innovation in its workforce and products. Depicted: Serpentine bronze™ design on Vessels™ Conical Bell lavatory.

While introducing new opportunities for community colleges to consider, these objectives also pose formidable challenges. It will not be easy to integrate arts and culture seamlessly into already dense and demanding curricula, most of which now focus on very practical skills or fulfilling university requirements. It will take supportive trustees and administrators to elevate the importance of the arts among the multiple missions of the institution. It will require patience to help local officials redefine arts and culture in economic development terms and to

This decorative piece was created by a student at the Galway-Mayo Institute of Technology's Furniture College in Letterfrack, Ireland. GMIT and a rural community development agency partnered to create the world-class college, which helped revive Ireland's furniture industry and reinvigorate the local economy.

- Enrich the colleges' learning environment.
- Enhance the occupational and social skills of students.
- Expand the economic opportunities available to the community and students.
- Contribute to a community's quality of life.

The second challenge will be convincing students (and counselors) that creativity is a skill that can be used in a variety of ways and one that will produce positive economic outcomes. Students and parents want practical skills for conventional career paths that have worked in the past. The arts, to skeptics, are the frosting, not the cake. It is rare, for instance, for states or nations to express concerns about skill shortages in the creative fields as they do about traditional occupations. The third challenge will be overcoming reluctance, often based on misconceptions and inadequate occupational data, to consider the employment and employability potential of arts and design students.

help students, guidance counselors, and parents understand the career pathways associated with arts and design and the institution's cultural impact on the community.

The first challenge will be overcoming the concern that increased attention and greater emphasis on the arts, design, and culture in the community college will add yet another mission to an already overextended institution. That is not the intent. The principles conveyed in this publication are meant to represent changes whose benefits are worth the risks and that will

Change will require a reassessment of the value of the arts and culture to work, community, and economy. The problem is nicely summed up by Italian composer Gian Carlo Menotti on a visit to the North Carolina Community College System: "The trouble with Americans is that you think the arts are an after-dinner mint! No, no, no! The arts, they are the bread of life!" (cited in Lancaster, 2004). In the United States, it may take the realization that arts are also the bread of industry to raise awareness and appreciation of the arts in all aspects of life and work.

2. Defining Creative Enterprises, Workers, and Communities

Until quite recently, few communities fully appreciated the economic development value or job potential of arts and culture. The public sector treated the arts as only marginally important to economic growth —and definitely not a significant wealth generator. In fact, most communities looked to charitable contributions for support of the arts. If there was any economic value in arts and culture, it was in making contributions to amenities and quality of life that could influence corporate investment decisions and attract tourists. In retrospect, it is clear that the arts and culture have produced positive economic outcomes. Because they were not embodied in companies captured by conventional economic analyses, however, their value has been underestimated.

The explosive response to the publication of *The Rise of the Creative Class* (Florida, 2002) moved the creative economy into the mainstream of public policy. A growing collection of research studies has convinced policymakers at the highest levels of government of the importance of art, design, and culture in a knowledge-based economy. Today nearly every nation and region strives—and even claims—to be a creative economy, home to talented, creative people and creative and design-intensive companies.

Communities strive to be cool places to live and work, with cultures and institutions that support diversity, tolerance, and creative expression. One state has made creative economies a gubernatorial priority. On January 25,

What Is a Creative Enterprise Cluster?

- Companies with products that consist of art or design (e.g., pottery, writing, jewelry, and Web page design)

- Companies that rely on art or design to be the distinguishing feature and competitive advantage of their products or services (e.g., high-fashion clothing, CDs, designer home furnishings, advertising, landscaping, and architecture)

- Companies that sell, supply, or contribute to art or design-dependent products or services (e.g., galleries, craft and supply distributors, and arts councils; arts or craft schools; and art foundries)

- Institutions and agencies that educate, assist, or support people or companies that produce or rely on art or design (e.g., colleges, universities, banks, and small-business centers)

Source: Rosenfeld (2004a).

2005, Maine's governor, John Baldacci, signed an executive order establishing the Maine Creative Economy Council and promising in his State of the State address the resources to back it up.

Creative enterprises—firms and entrepreneurs that rely on a continuous flow of new ideas and innovations from creative people and institutions—constitute the core of creative economies. Creative communities are places with the kinds of recreational and cultural amenities and creative milieus that attract talent, which in turn fuels a creative economy. When certain types of creative people, enterprises, and institutions tend to converge geographically, they become "creative clusters," which is one of

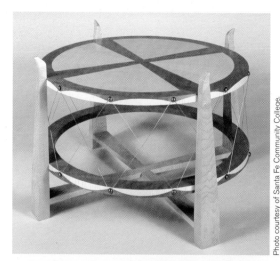

This table was designed and produced by a student in Santa Fe (NM) Community College's fine woodworking program.

the current policy frameworks for understanding regional economies and setting policy. Clusters are places with relatively high concentrations (compared with national or state averages) of similar or complementary companies and institutions. The major distinction between creative economies and creative clusters is that the former is a set of companies, whereas the latter describes an ecosystem that benefits from proximity to and relationships with customers, suppliers, agents, distributors, cooperatives, support services, and education institutions.

Both creative economies and creative clusters are difficult to define, much less understand, because few of the enterprises are officially classified according to the creative content of their products or services. No country has an industry or occupational classification scheme that uses creativity as a distinguishing characteristic (with the exception of the arts themselves). Yet even with varying definitions, there is surprisingly close agreement on the scale, impact, and growth of the creative economy. Studies from around the world show that the creative economy represents about a 4% to 5% share of total employment, a 3% to 8% of GNP, and an annual growth rate of 6% to 10%. Yet because of the absence of standard classifications and a tendency to be conservative and use defensible definitions, and because the economy is populated by large numbers of microenterprises and people that are undercounted in conventional data collections, the size and impacts of the cluster are usually underestimated.

Photo courtesy of Santa Fe Community College.

Jeff Little, director of the new Larry Gatlin School of Entertainment Technology at Guilford Technical Community College in High Point, North Carolina, shows one of its control rooms to members of the Media Arts Alliance.

Products With Pizzazz

Which companies are sufficiently dependent on the artistic content of their products or services to be considered a creative enterprise and included in the creative economy? Capturing the size and potential economic impact of the creative sector is much more difficult than it is for traditional sectors of the economy. The universe of creative enterprises includes those that produce art and design and those that use it to compete. One part of the first set of firms lends itself more easily to classification. Most definitions of creative economies include art and performance, advertising, architecture, film and video, radio and television, writing and publishing, graphic design, leisure software, art dealers and galleries, interior design, and ornamental woodwork and metalwork.

Most craft firms—as well as performers, freelance designers, and writers—are small, independent companies made up of the artist and perhaps a few apprentices or journeymen. They may not be recognized in terms of economic development except as a tourist attraction. Very small businesses may not be captured by national employer databases maintained by employment security commissions or by the government in records of companies that do not have paid employees. They may not be recorded by U.S. census occupation, especially if they have other jobs to support themselves as they develop their careers. Collectively, however, they may constitute a significant proportion of the employment and growth in the economy. Across the United States, for example, 30% of the total number of people officially employed as artists and performers are self-employed, and many more report too little income to be classified at all or are misclassified as part of a more expansive manufacturing sector.

A second group of commonly overlooked creative enterprise employers includes businesses classified in traditional sectors but that derive their principal competitive advantage from the artistic content or design of their products or services. Some are at the fringes of the arts and crafts sector, producing at scale but using art and design as their product mark. These companies compete by producing objects or services that are purchased for their aesthetics, typically sold at a higher price than equally functional items that lack the aesthetic value.

Imaginative Workers

Most occupational education is intended to teach creative problem-solving and decision-making skills. There are, in fact, few classes of occupations and few types of businesses that do not include and cannot benefit from some degree of creativity. A recent detailed study of the work lives of so-called low-skilled employees illustrates the ingenuity and creativity they have to draw on daily just to do their jobs effectively (Rose, 2004). The majority of the occupations listed in the O*NET database have some requirements for problem-solving skills, which imply creativity.

For the purposes of this book, however, *creativity* refers to the ability to express oneself artistically. It is not the broader definition of creativity as originality and imagination, which could legitimately be applied to many fields, including science and engineering. The occupational classifications used by Richard Florida, for example, include scientists, technicians, and health-care workers. Official classifications, once again, are inadequate for defining arts- or design-based occupations. The most obvious occupations—artist, musician, or architect, for example—have been assigned codes, but there is no way to distinguish between the producer of hand-built pottery or blown glass from the manufacturer of mass-produced ceramic or glass products.

Students prepare animation projects at the Glamorgan Centre for Art and Design Technology at Coleg Morgannwg in Wales. Students begin by learning handicrafts and then progress to digital skills.

The college transformed a historic grammar school in Pontypridd. The Centre is now a leading source of artists and animators.

Photos courtesy of Coleg Morgannwg.

My definition of creative work is that set of competencies that must include forms of expression that are associated with arts and design, that generate images, forms, sounds, or words that bring visceral, behavioral, or reflective enjoyment to consumers, users, or audiences. It is the creativity generally associated with the right side of the brain rather than the systemic and analytical skills associated with the left side. This definition does not restrict the creative economy to artists, performers, and crafts people. It includes traditional industries that take their competitive advantage from art, design, or novelty; commercial industries that use art and design, such as architecture, landscaping, and advertising; media and entertainment industries that depend on creativity, arts, and design such as Web design and content, digital gaming, and animation; and even cosmetology—a program of vocational education studies that many students choose for the opportunity to be artistic, entrepreneurial, and independent (Florida, 2002). Not only are these occupations of significant size, but most are growing faster than the national average for all jobs (see Table 1).

Clusters of Creative Companies

The current most popular economic entity of choice used to define and develop regional economies is the "industry cluster." Creative enterprises also tend to cluster and thus represent a legitimate target for economic and skill development. A cluster includes not only companies but also the institutions and organiza-

Cool Community Colleges   **13**

tions that support them, including community and technical colleges, nonprofit organizations, special schools, and business and professional associations. Firms cluster because they benefit from the externalities that come from scale, that is, availability of specialized services, bankers, accountants familiar with their businesses, access to knowledge and information, and—perhaps the most important—a proficient and experienced labor force. Creative enterprises and people choose to locate near other creative people for inspiration and problem solving; to be in a supportive work environment; to be a member of a strong and active arts council; to be able to network for more efficient production, marketing, or purchasing; or to reach a scale that attracts more customers.

In some places, clusters are self-evident because they have developed a reputation or local brand. Some build on traditions that go back centuries; others are relatively young, resulting from skills passed down through generations and shared with friends and neighbors or growing from institutional settings such as crafts schools. The following arts-based regions illustrate creative clusters.

- Seagrove, North Carolina, population 246, and the surrounding towns are home to more than 100 potteries. The cluster can date its roots back to immigrants from Stratfordshire, England, who made and sold pottery for everyday use. Jugtown Pottery was among the first companies to successfully turn the skill into an art form. Today, the clay programs at North Carolina's Montgomery Community College (which produce new entrepreneurs), the North Carolina Pottery Center (which exhibits students' work), and the local government offices all support the cluster.

- A quarter of the employment base of Taos, New Mexico, call themselves artists, one of the highest concentrations in the United States. Ninety art galleries line the streets of this town of only 5,000. Artists gravitated there in the 1920s, forming the Taos Society of Artists and attracting many more estab-

Table 1. Scale and Growth of Selected Creative Occupations in the United States

Occupation	Employment 2002 (in thousands)	Projected Growth, 2002–2012
Fine artists, animators, multimedia specialists	775	16.1%
Musicians and composers	215	16.2%
Writers and editors	319	16.0%
Architects	113	17.3%
Landscape architects	23	22.2%
Graphic designers	212	21.9%
Interior designers	60	21.7%
Media equipment specialists	295	16.9%
Film and video editors	19	26.4%
Cabinetmakers	147	9.4%

Source: Hecker (2004)

lished and would-be artists. In addition to the galleries, Taos has seven museums, a performing arts theater, annual film festival, and numerous writers and poets. The Taos Art Association, lecture series, and a strong social infrastructure form a supportive environment for the cluster. Nearby Northern New Mexico Community College and Santa Fe Community College offer an array of arts-based programs including fiber arts, fine furniture, and graphic arts.

- The southern part of Manhattan is home to a large new media cluster that includes companies that produce Web-based services and systems used by established New York City industries (printing, publishing, entertainment, finance, and advertising) to communicate, market, and transmit creative content. As in many art and design-based clusters, it is difficult to identify members because many are classified as advertising or publishing companies. Support comes from the New York New Media Association, the city's community colleges (with internship programs and media centers) and universities, and design institutes.

Creative clusters also exist across Europe and, in fact, many of the most noted industrial clusters of Italy owe their success to the incorporation of art, culture, and history into their products, and their technical schools are key assets (Bettoli & Micelli, 2005).

- Maniago, Italy, called the cutlery city of Italy, is a small town with about 120 companies making fine, artistically designed cutlery for all purposes. The art and design are part of the overall shape, unique handles, engraved blades, and packaging. The cluster is sustained by a local technical college with specialized metalworking and apprenticeship programs, collective marketing, a cutlery museum, shops that attract tourists, and an industry association.

- Grottaglie, a small town in the heel of the boot of Italy, has designated a significant sector of the city as its Ceramics Quarter. Street after street of potters practice their art, producing quality and quantity that can be exported all over the world. The city has a ceramic museum and training programs, and the city uses ceramics as its brand and major tourist attraction.

- The economy of Vorarlberg, the westernmost region of Austria, has a high concentration of textile manufacturing. A segment that specializes in embroidery and fine lace—more than 600 small firms—is tightly clustered around the city of Lustenau. The companies use similar technologies, have similar products, and target the same markets, and all that distinguishes one firm from another is design. The Chamber of Commerce (which is responsible for workforce development) supplies information, lobbies, and operates a Wi-Fi (wireless fidelity) training facility (one of Austria's regional training centers). The textile school in Dornbirn is responsible for ensuring a skilled workforce.

Many other places have creative clusters that are less specialized, with large concentrations of cross-pollinated artists and other creative enterprises. Parts of western North Carolina, the Montana Rockies, the Berkshires of western Massachusetts, Washington's Olympic Peninsula, and the Maine coast fit this bill. Others exist, such as the 500-plus art glass manufacturers in Seattle, Washington, but are largely unnoticed because even collectively they compose too small a part of a large urban economy.

Portraits of Creative Economies

It is time for community colleges to pay more attention to the creativity of their students and in their economies because

1. Arts- and crafts-based enterprises collectively produce significant wealth.

2. Those firms most likely to continue to produce goods in the United States will be based on technology, fashion, or design.

3. Creative communities attract talent and good jobs.

4. Talent exists across geographic, racial, ethnic, and class boundaries.

5. Community colleges can have a major influence on creativity in people, businesses, and communities.

To set parameters for defining creative economies, examples are available from around the world to establish a framework for measuring scale and impact.

Creative Clusters in New England

A landmark study of New England creative clusters, the Creative Economy Initiative, set the standards for measuring creative economies. Sponsored by the New England Council and carried out by Mt. Auburn Associates, Phase 1 of the study (New England Council, 2000) used a somewhat conservative definition of creative cluster that included literary arts, media, heritage, performing arts, visual arts, applied arts, and support industries. The study showed that the cluster accounted for about 3.5% of New England's total employment base and had a much faster growth rate than the region's overall economy. The study also revealed that 40% of New England's creative workers are self-employed.

In 2001, the Council issued *The Creative Economy Initiative: A Blueprint for Investment in New England's Creative Economy,* which recommended 10 action initiatives under the following four goals:

1. Creative New England seeks to promote the sustainable economic development of New England's culture-based creative economy so that it may fully contribute to regional economic competitiveness and quality of life.

2. Creative cluster aims to generate new jobs and economic activity by increasing the growth, vitality, and competitiveness of New England's creative cluster.

3. Creative workforce will strengthen and expand New England's creative workforce by promoting understanding, awareness, opportunities, and access to training and employment in the creative occupations.

4. Creative communities will enhance the economic and social quality of life in New England communities by fostering a rich arts and cultural environment. (New England Council, 2001)

The Council pointed out that community colleges, with their experience in workforce development, especially in serving low-income populations and nontraditional students, have the potential to foster a creative workforce and are in a position to help shape policy. The study and blueprint help show that, as workforce development leaders, community colleges must play a key role in working with creative industries to establish a presence on the state economic development agenda.

HandMade in America

Recognizing in the early 1990s that the kind of manufacturing western North Carolina had had was not going to return and that the region needed a new vision, Rebecca Anderson founded HandMade in America, which has become an internationally renowned and award-winning engine for economic development. Having learned the language and techniques of economic developers during her prior work at the Chamber of Commerce, Anderson had the experience to be an effective intermediary between the arts and economic development camps. HandMade documented, for example, an economic impact to the economy of $122 million, more than either tobacco or furniture, and, by analyzing downtown real estate, showed that the creative sector's value was $65 million.

Fabric art by Hocking College (Nelsonville, Ohio) student Bambi Taylor.

One of HandMade's earliest and biggest successes was the publication of *The Craft Heritage Trails of Western North Carolina* (Fields, 2003), a visually attractive, easy-to-use guide intended to bring consumers to artists, artisans, and art attractions. Now in its third printing, it has sold about 50,000 copies and attracted 21,000 visitors, 70% of whom spent more than $100 on arts or crafts. Anderson was also instrumental in starting, in cooperation with Mayland Community College (NC), the Energy-Xchange, which consists of an artisan and agricultural incubator and studios that get their energy from the methane released from a landfill and is now being replicated in two other counties. HandMade operates marketing and tourism management workshops and arts business institutes and is beginning an apprenticeship program and design center incubator.

Montana's Creative Cluster

One study that identified and mapped Montana's creative enterprise cluster relied heavily on local knowledge, such as membership lists of arts organizations and foundations and on product descriptions from industry directories (Rosenfeld, 2004b). In this large, rural state, official government data for employers missed more than half of the people in this cluster earning all or a significant part of their income from arts- and design-related business. Montana was among the first states to see the economic potential of creative enterprises and their derivatives in other parts of the economy. It led to a creative enterprise cluster position in the governor's office and new efforts to expand both the marketing capacity and entrepreneurial skills of the cluster. For example, the cluster took an exhibit of Montana art to Ireland, which resulted in sales of other non-arts products and built trade relationships, and worked with the College of Technology in Great Falls to develop new markets for Native American arts.

Digital Creativity in Scotland

Although Scotland embarked on a cluster strategy in the mid-1990s, the idea of a creative economy cluster faced considerable opposition from other sectors that worried that calling some industries creative would make it appear that others were uncreative. Scotland settled on a definition in which creativity was not just an agent of change but more like a raw material that industries processed into salable goods and services. Scotland's creative cluster includes in its core content originators, distributors, and markets. Its partners include industry associations, colleges and universities, libraries and museums, and government agencies. (The connection to the colleges led to a recent plan for workforce development for audiovisual industries.) The full cluster supports 70,000 to 100,000 jobs and contributes $8 billion to the economy, which is about 4% of Scotland's GNP (Tibbetts, 2004).

3. Gaining Recognition and Acceptance for Creative Occupations

The arts are not new to community colleges. Virtually all colleges offer some credit and continuing education courses in the arts. So why all the excitement today? Perhaps it is because in the past, appreciation for the arts and culture has largely been limited to their contributions to local culture, for their intrinsic value to the whole person, as a liberal arts education path, or for hobbyists. They have not been fully embraced as occupational paths or as a means of economic development. Colleges may proudly showcase the products of talented students in lobbies, offices, exhibits, and performances, but if these talents are not also valued for their employment and economic potential, they remain peripheral to colleges' core mission.

That view, however, is far too limited. Demand for jobs in technology-based occupations that incorporate arts and design, such as graphic art, Web design, computer game design, animation, and architecture, is growing faster than the national average rate of job growth. Colleges that have discovered the economic value of the more traditional arts, design, and culture to their students, economies, and communities and the contributions of the arts to learning and creativity have reordered their priorities.

North Carolina Community College System

Students working toward their Art and Design Foundation Studies Diploma at the Centre for Design and Creative Technologies, Limavady College of Further and Higher Education in Northern Ireland.

Photo courtesy of Stuart Rosenfeld.

Links Across the Atlantic

Finlandia University's contribution to the creative economy is a step in a decade-long effort by Northern Economic Initiatives Corporation (NEIC) to use art and design to resuscitate the economy of Michigan's Northern Peninsula. When it lost its largest employer, Hancock Air Force Base, the county was forced to turn back to its roots and its wood products industry. NEIC recognized that to compete, the industry was going to have to move upscale and that the best way to make it part of the local culture was to get it into the school system.

The large Finnish population in the county provided the opportunity. NEIC began by establishing an alliance between Suomi College, a century-old two-year college in Hancock with declining enrollments, and the Kuopio Academy of Design in Finland, to organize exchanges among faculty, students, and community leaders. Suomi began a business-based Finnish design program. One outcome was the International School of Art and Design at Suomi College, which has reorganized and renamed itself Finlandia University. The school emphasizes ceramics, glass, fiber and fashion design, product and interior design, and graphic and digital design. Its latest innovation is to strengthen the business side of the sector by increasing access to IT, adding a Design Service Center, and including a business incubator in the new arts and design center located in a former hospital.

President Martin Lancaster (2004) remarked on the importance of arts and culture to creativity, college, and the community:

> We [in the community colleges] must cultivate the spark of creativity that everyone has and turn it into the habit of originality….In community colleges, we must also commit to recognizing that the exercise of creativity is in itself a legitimate way to make a living….In our community colleges we must support artists and thinkers in their work. We must teach the arts across our curriculum. We must sponsor exhibits, performances, festivals, contests and other events founded on creativity as part of our role as "conveners of public life."

Some colleges are already responding to the creative interests and needs of students and communities:

- Haywood Community College in western North Carolina has had crafts programs since 1974 that have graduated and supported generations of successful business people and large numbers of new enterprises.

- Northern California's College of the Redwoods has graduated and dispersed makers of fine furniture across the nation while at the same time supporting its local cluster of high-end furniture producers.

- Central Carolina Community College's Siler City campus in North Carolina has an arts incubator with 33 tenant businesses and almost as many on the waiting list, with a goal of 200.

• Wallace State Community College in Hanceville, Alabama, in 2004 was given a museum collection valued at $9.5 million, which it intends to locate in a new Fine and Performing Arts Center scheduled to open in spring 2007.

• Mountain Empire Community College in southwestern Virginia received an Appalachian Regional Commission grant to establish the Mountain Music School, banking on its traditional music to revive its economy through tourism. The school will begin as a summer program but expects to grow into a year-round program.

Three general themes reflect the different types of impact that community colleges can have:

1. Embedding arts, design, and culture into the curricula and institution (intended to help students learn and earn a living).

2. Supporting the business of arts and design (aimed at making local companies more competitive and entrepreneurial).

3. Delivering arts and culture to the community (to make communities more desirable and attractive places to live and work).

Photo courtesy of Haywood Community College Professional Crafts.

Exhibit in 2005 at Blue Spiral, one of Asheville's finest art and craft galleries, by students from Haywood Community College's crafts programs.

Solutions to Persistent Problems Through the Arts

The Harlan campus of the Southeast Kentucky Community and Technical College sits in the heart of one of America's persistently poorest regions. Poverty and lack of hope have resulted in alcohol and drug abuse, crime, domestic and civil violence, and debt. Yet in the face of this adversity, the area h as retained a strong cultural identity based on its tradition of storytelling, music, and crafts and a shared desire to recapture its historical strengths. With a grant from the Rockefeller Foundation, the college set out to build on the region's artistic and cultural assets to address economic and social problems.

Southeast initiated "scanning bees" to preserve digital images of historic photographs, collected historic documents, worked with the Kentucky Foundation for Women to create exhibitions of photographs and paintings celebrating mountain women, and, in partnership with the Kentucky Arts Council, sponsored community residencies with muralists and creative writers. During the first 15 months of the project, 900 county residents took part in at least one residency. One exhibit featured 240 Harlan County photographers who also wrote about their photographs. Participants in another project made ceramic tiles with the intent of creating a large permanent public work of art designed by local people. Still other projects featured story gathering and listening. The project, still under way, is a moving example of a college attracting the resources to raise cultural awareness, teach skills, generate pride in place, and overcome some of the social problems that have prevented economic growth.

Embedding Arts and Design in Curricula, Institutions, and Economies

The artistic talent of potential employees, for many years considered by employers to be an outside interest or hobby, is now considered a desirable skill and a decided advantage. The arts foster the kind of creativity many new economy companies are—and traditional companies should be—seeking, and which community colleges should be teaching. Employers increasingly want the right-brain skills that are associated with the arts for a wide range of jobs. A recent article in *WIRED* magazine contended that "any job that can be reduced to a set of rules is at risk." Tomorrow's economy, it predicts, will be dominated by "high concept, high touch" jobs that involve the ability to create artistic and emotional beauty, to detect patterns and opportunities, to craft a satisfying narrative, and to come up with inventions that the world didn't know it was missing" (Pink, 2005). A graduate of a Vermont community college auto body program was hired by a clockmaker because of the artistic talent he developed in his welding class. Yet students in that class were unable to admit they were creative; they were "just" welders.

The connection between art and technology is most obvious in the fast-growing digital industries that make up the creative enterprise cluster, such as new media, film, music, Web-based advertising, and animation and is also evident in advertising, architecture, and landscaping. In these industries, talents are valued as highly as skills, which can be more easily learned. For example, artistic students at the Glamorgan Centre of Art and Design Technology, part of Coleg Morgannwg in Wales, are recruited heavily by new-media companies such as Pixar Animation Studios, The Walt Disney Company, and the British Broadcasting Corporation (BBC).

Employers of more traditional manufacturing and service industries have shown less interest in artistic talent, although that may be changing as they realize they need to be creative in order to distinguish themselves from competitors. A half-century ago, British industry was urged to bring art and design into its factories to compete with imports from countries that were offering higher fashions. The weakness of British industry, according to noted educator Herbert Read (1953) in *Art in Industry,* was that it was "run for the most part by people who have no understanding of the meaning of art, and no inclination to resign any of their functions to the artist."

American industry today may be facing similar challenges, except the success of imports is based on cost advantages, not art. The United States has already lost large shares of jobs in consumer electronics, furniture, textiles, and apparel. One firm that has found an answer in a very threatened industry is Munro and Company in Hot Springs, Arkansas. Munro created a niche for itself through art and now is one of America's last surviving shoe companies (with half of all U.S. shoe production). By producing specialty shoes and accessories, some of which incorporate fine art, the firm is able to reach a loyal, high-end customer base. By bringing in artists to work with employees to paint murals

Photos courtesy of Coleg Morgannwg.

Galway-Mayo Institute of Technology's Furniture College is located in a former boys' reformatory in a village in the northwestern corner of Connemara, Ireland. A GMIT student combines advanced production technologies with art to make products.

on the walls, creating a visually pleasing environment, and by adding recreational facilities to each plant (even a nine-hole golf course), the company has maintained high productivity and low turnover (Williams, 2004).

Ireland's Galway-Mayo Institute of Technology (GMIT) takes advantage of the arts in its programs but also applies the arts to its institutional setting. The design of GMIT's new Learning Centre integrated aesthetics and functionality so that graduates are characterized by their profes-

Traditional music is integral to many creative economies, particularly in Appalachia and the Mississippi Delta. Mountain Empire Community College in Virginia and Hazard Community and Technical College in Kentucky are creating centers around musical heritage.

sional and applied orientation and creative abilities. GMIT has a successful art and design program—paint, print, ceramics, sculpture, and textile design—that attracts the highest number of mature applicants for the institute and for the first Heritage program in the country. GMIT promotes the idea that creativity should not be defined by traditional boundaries, and even scientists and engineers are discovering there is much they can learn from the pedagogy of arts and design. The institute has developed educational partnerships with community arts organizations, which simultaneously address the regional development mission and demands of students and industry (Coy, 2004).

GMIT's furniture production program in the village of Letterfrack, Ireland, represents one of the best examples of the integration of art and design into technical education. Each person who applies to the program is expected to submit a portfolio demonstrating artistic talents. The Furniture College started in 1989 as an ambitious joint venture between GMIT and a community-based development agency. Its plan was to take an abandoned reformatory for boys in a poor, rural part of Connemara and make it into a world-class college that could use art and design to revive Ireland's furniture industry and reinvigorate the local economy. It has had success on both scores, growing from a handful of students to 175, from a single certificate program to multiple certificate, diploma, and degree programs in, for example, furniture design and manufacture and furniture production, furniture conservation and restoration, and furniture technology. Graduates and faculty introduced technical and design principles into Irish companies and brought a youthful vigor to the community. Its talented students produce fine furniture that is exhibited and sold across Europe (Rosenfeld, 2001).

The creative sectors themselves, which need imagination to function, are setting the pace for education. Nigel Paine, head of People Development at the BBC in London, has described BBC as a "learning environment with creativity at the heart," a place that assumes "everyone has solutions." BBC has 26,000 employees and is responsible for half of the United Kingdom's media exports. It is London's largest creative enterprise. In 2004, BBC's Training and Development provided 3,814 courses for more than

22,000 people and 5,000 hours of online learning within and outside BBC. Like most creative industries, Paine said, "BBC lives on prototypes, not production," which is challenging for a large bureaucracy. Therefore, it is constantly challenged to reinvent itself (Paine, 2004).

Bellingham Technical College (BTC) in Washington brought art into an unlikely place—the college's welding program. Making art produced more skilled welders, taught teamwork, opened the door to new economic opportunities, and focused the attention of local employers on design. The initiative began with a welded sculpture competition among the 120 students, called "Junkyards War" (see cover photo). Students sell the pieces at a silent auction—some have sold for thousands of dollars. Its 2005 competition drew competitors from technical colleges in Denmark and Scotland. The college is now part of a larger community effort that includes the local university's industrial design and art and sculpture program, other BTC manufacturing programs, and local development and tourism agencies (Pumphrey, 2004).

Last—but not at all least—the arts and design expand access to nontraditional learners and underserved populations. Despite the accessibility, open door policies, and low costs of community colleges, large numbers of potential students who could benefit do not. They may stay away because they lack confidence, dislike the academic environment, or see nothing there that interests them enough to make the effort.

There is a certain segment of potential students, however, who might be attracted by

Turning Traditions Into Jobs

The Appalachian Mountain regions of Kentucky, home to some of the nation's economically distressed communities, have been looking for decades for opportunities to create good jobs without giving up their culture. By 1997, the percentage of completers for both high school diplomas and bachelor's degrees in Knott County lagged behind the state and national averages, and the population was declining as young people left. With little hope of attracting a growing, large high-tech company, residents of Knott County turned to one of their most prized but underused assets, their rich endowment of talent in the arts, music, and handcrafts.

Hazard Community and Technical College wanted to purchase the historic Hindman High School and convert it into the Kentucky School of Craft. The school, approved and funded by the Commonwealth in 1998, opened in 2004 with the governor's support. The school will offer degree programs and short-term training in wood, jewelry/metals, ceramics, fibers, and blacksmithing. It emphasizes the business of crafts, integrating entrepreneurial skills and hosting a business enterprise center, studio residency program, and cooperative studio building with shared equipment. It involves youth through the two-week summer Appalachian Adventure Art Camp and NorthStar. The school not only helps the community economy but also gives young people new options to connect with the community and become leaders who can sustain it for years to come.

college programs that take forms of expression —art, design, or music—and turn them into environments for learning and gateways to careers. The arts and design, if marketed properly, could attract students who, for financial or other reasons, may not have considered becoming a college student. For example, only 1 of the 21 students enrolled in Montana State University-Great Falls College of Technology's regional artisans program this year is what colleges think of as a traditional student. Thirteen have hardship scholarships, 13 are from very rural areas or small towns, 18 are over 30, and 12 had been working at their craft for more than 10 years.

Addressing Business Imperatives

Many artists and artisans are not seeking employment but need to be able to earn a living in order to make their talents and passions their lives' work. These are the artisan–entrepreneurs who produce functional and artistic pieces, some of which may simply be on display, but many of which serve useful purposes in homes or offices. They may be potters, weavers, glass blowers, visual artists, or writers. Others may make fine furniture, fashion apparel, custom jewelry, or home furnishings. Some may want to handcraft objects one at a time; others may want to scale up to meet larger market demands. Some handcrafters make one-of-a-kind pieces or, more often, replicate successful products and sell them in galleries, at shows, or on the Internet.

In the early part of the 20th century, an arts and crafts movement prospered across the United States and Europe, and there was a market for high-quality goods. The renowned architect Walter Gropius once lamented that "the transformation from manual to machine production so preoccupied humanity for a century that instead of pressing forward to tackle the real problems of design, men were content with borrowed styles and conventional decorations" (cited in Read, 1953).

There appears to be a resurgence of the arts and crafts movement, although it is not likely to take the same form. Today technology makes it much easier to customize designs and experiment with styles, but education in design has been oriented toward efficiency and performance and has neglected originality and style. Moreover, there is some backlash against mass-marketed goods and an increasing desire for authenticity and originality, as is witnessed by the rapid growth of Whole Foods Market and other grocers that feature locally grown foods and the popularity of boutique galleries and arts and craft fairs. The export value of the U.S. music and entertainment industry is larger than that of many traditional manufacturing sectors.

At most colleges, these creative sectors of the economy have been largely marginalized because their potential for economic success is not taken into account in employment projections that drive program planning and resources. Artisanal businesses are most likely to be found in the government databases of establishments without employees or mixed in with other craft industry codes. Industry classification schemes do not distinguish between firms that mass-produce goods from those that handcraft artistic products. Artisan firms are not well served by manufacturing extension, cooperative extension service, or venture capital programs in the United States. The challenge for community colleges is to hone the talents of students in these fields, expose them to new techniques and technologies, and also make sure they get the requisite business skills to become successful entrepreneurs and small business owners.

Montgomery Community College, located in one of the nation's premier ceramics clusters at Seagrove, North Carolina, began a pottery program in 1967 and began offering a degree in 1971. More than 1,700 students have gone through the college's clay programs, and as its reputation grew it began attracting students from all over the world. The college has a gallery and show for students' thesis projects. When the program began, the craft already had been practiced in the area for centuries, but there were only a small number of potteries. The growth in Seagrove from a dozen or so potteries in the 1970s to more than 100 today was energized by graduates of the college, 38 of whom started new businesses. The college uses REAL Enterprises, a national program in which students start and operate businesses, to encourage entrepreneurship. In a county with low levels of education and a declining traditional manufacturing base, pottery is a growing part of the economy and is turning into a major tourist attraction.

Hazard Community and Technical College (HCC), located in an economically distressed

Embedded in the New Economic Landscape—College of the Redwoods

The economy of rural Humboldt County, California, depends on natural resources, craft industries, and lifestyle to attract tourists and discourage young people from leaving. The College of the Redwoods' Eureka campus has the primary responsibility for training the workforce and supporting the local economy. When California identified its key clusters, natural resource industries dominated the economic landscape, but both arts and culture and manufacturing also ranked high; the two clusters intersected at industrial design. The arts provided competitive advantages to many craft-based manufacturing subclusters, such as play equipment, jewelry, furniture, gourmet foods, and musical instruments.

When the region formulated its Prosperity! Network, arts and culture were among the cornerstones. The community college, which has had a nationally known program in fine woodworking since 1981, was well positioned to support an arts and culture cluster. Its fine furniture program, which has its own elephant and chisel logo as its brand, has graduates working in 36 states, but 79 stayed in northern California. The college also now offers a violin- and bow-making institute plus a degree program and continuing education in historic preservation and restoration technology—the only one west of the Mississippi. The college was recently invited by a nearby former mill town to help with restoration of the town. For 15 years, the College of the Redwoods has hosted a national three-day "celebration of wood" called WoodFair, and the college is planning a National Folk Music Instrument Institute.

area in Kentucky's Appalachian Mountains, turned to arts and craft to create jobs without giving up its local culture. The Commonwealth of Kentucky approved HCC's conversion of the historic Hindman High School at HCC's Knott County Branch into the Kentucky School of Craft, and it enrolled its first students in 2004. The goal of the school is to train people to start and expand craft and craft related businesses that create high quality works based on the regional traditions of design and workmanship. Developing crafts as businesses, director Tim Glotzbach emphasizes, is critical to the school's regional economic goals. Programs are fused with entrepreneurial skills, and the school includes a business enterprise center, a shared equipped cooperative studio, and business incubator.

New Brunswick College of Craft and Design in Fredericton (Canada) was founded in 1938 to teach crafts as a means for the agricultural and fisheries sectors to earn supplemental income during the winter months, but its focus gradually shifted toward students who wanted to be full-time artisans. New Brunswick's cultural and fisheries industries are the seventh-largest sector in the economy and growing; therefore it has become a high priority for economic development policy in this relatively poor province and holds the key to the sector's growth and prosperity. Enrollments at the college waned in the 1970s and 1980s, because graduates were unable to earn enough money to support their talents. In the 1990s, the college responded by adding marketing and entrepreneurial skills to the curricula and by

changing entrance and graduation requirements to reflect the new focus. Today the college has certificate and diploma programs in clay, creative graphics, textiles, jewelry and metal arts, surface design, and native arts studies. In March 2005, the college hosted a Canada-wide Crafts Marketing Conference to help artists expand their markets (Kavanagh, 2004).

Blazing Career Paths Through Creative Economies

Among the barriers to greater recognition and acceptance of creative occupations is lack of a clear scheme for classifying them, insufficient understanding of market demand or career paths, and absence of generally accepted skill standards or occupational competencies. This applies to most craft-based or creative industries. South Africa's educational agency recognizes the creative arts with a formal national skills development strategy, similar to other key sectors of the economy.

The standards, used by South Africa's Technikons and Further Education and Training colleges and also by nongovernment agencies that work in disadvantaged communities, apply to theater, dance, music, arts and crafts, multimedia production, film and video, services for events, and arts and culture management. South Africa places the learner at the center of the system and defines competencies, but it also recognizes prior learning and sets criteria for measuring competencies achieved. Most of the training is completed in less than a year and includes basic fundamentals, core skills, and electives that give students qualifications—including business skills. Traditionally, art in the schools focused on expressive rather than technical skills. Now that the system is outcome based, art curricula also integrate instruction on marketing and practical use of skills.

TRACE (Transforming Regional Artisans into Creative Enterprises) is a new program for artisans at the Montana State University-Great Falls College of Technology. The college (also part of CraftNet—see page 31) designed this new program to support the state's efforts to grow its creative enterprise cluster. The program draws students from rural communities across the region and is designed to help artisans improve their business and marketing skills so they can be more successful without leaving the state. The one-year credit program, which began in 2005 as a pilot with 20 students, includes modules in arts marketing, creative entrepreneurship, Montana ways, Internet essentials, and "making it."

Over the past century, industrialized regions grew or made things that could be sold to other places in order to create wealth and prosperity. Until about the 1930s, production was a craft carried out by small, tightly networked shops with niche markets—and their competitive advantages—based on their finely honed skills and designs. Shortly before midcentury, the manufacturing base shifted into high gear and toward more standardized products in which costs were a principal competitive advantage. The arts and crafts production base became marginalized as a source of employment and wealth.

Photo courtesy of Claire Emery/Cindy Kittredge.

The roots of the word *manufacture* are *hand* and *make*. Many nations still refer to their small niche manufacturers in craft terms. Italy calls its small manufacturers artisan firms, and Germany refers to them as the handicrafts trade. In Germany, the term *handicraft* refers not to a product but to the scale of enterprise and skills of the manager. Enterprises in the handicraft trades are small firms managed by master craftsmen who are artists in their profession, expert in technical, design, and business skills (West German Chamber of Handicrafts Association, 1989).

The Art of Fine Wine

Walla Walla, a small city in southern Washington near the Oregon border whose economy had been based on agriculture, had been losing its jobs, its young people, and its hope. It needed a new niche to carry it into the 21st century. The region had operated vineyards since the early 19th century, but a combination of distance from the major railroad lines and some cold winters had kept production low, and the industry lay dormant. In 2000, Walla Walla Community College seized an opportunity to take advantage of the growing market for good wine in the United States. After operating an institute for three years, in 2003 the college opened its 15,000 square-foot Center for Enology and Viticulture—the first teaching commercial winery in Washington State. Planned with the expertise of eight of the valley's most experienced vintners, the center is contributing to and supporting the cluster's explosive growth—from 19 wineries in 1981 to 240 in 2003. The college also intends for the effort to have a wider effect, for example, spurring a renewed interest in art purveyors, community theater, tourism, and the hospitality industry. The wine industry, when combined with fine food and art purveyors, affords an enhanced opportunity for economic growth in the community. With the college leading the way, partnerships with other nearby colleges and universities, the state wine commission, Blue Mountain Arts Alliance, and valley restaurants exemplify the breadth of the effort.

Photo courtesy of Kentucky School of Craft.

The Kentucky School of Craft at Hazard Community and Technical College was selected by the governor of Kentucky as a special site for training master artisans and using the arts to revitalize the economy. The college converted the historic Hindman High School into the school, opened in 2004, and now offers AAS degrees in five areas.

Delivering Arts and Culture to Communities

Chain store malls, fast food restaurants, and interstate highways have taken the business out of downtown and the soul out of many communities, replacing the individuality of places with standardization. A counter movement is emerging to help communities redefine themselves and revive their cultural heritage—in part because of changing tastes of employees and employers and because of the expanding efforts to attract tourists to replace declines in manufacturing.

States and regions are discovering the economic benefits of community art, culture, recreational amenities, and an open, tolerant atmosphere (Florida, 2002). Maine Governor John Baldacci's stated vision is "building Maine communities through the arts." People are drawn to Maine, he said, "by its many craftsmen and for visits to Maine's historic sites, villages, and museums" (Baldacci, 2004, 2005).

Community colleges should be, and in some places already are, contributing to or even leading the way for building cultural awareness and creative communities. The best of the colleges have helped reinvent and redesign their communities and economies, as the following examples illustrate.

Moraine Valley Community College in Illinois has a Fine and Performing Arts Center with 575- and 150-seat theaters, an art gallery, and an atrium to showcase student, staff, and community art; it represents a major cultural center for the southwest suburbs of Chicago. Iowa Western Community College in Council Bluffs has a 660-seat theater for imported and community college performances and concerts. Sierra College in California has a natural history museum, a nature trail, the Center for Sierra Nevada Studies, the Ridley Art Gallery, and a theater, and it features annually a cabaret series, a madrigal feast, a spring festival, and concerts.

Walla Walla Community College in Washington turned the area's economy around using wine, art, and food (VanAusdle, 2004). Cape Cod Community College in Massachusetts is home to the Tilden Arts Center, which offers the community a full schedule of performances, plays, art presentations, and exhibits, all supported by its degree programs in music, theater, dance, and visual arts. In Bridgeport,

Collective Learning and Innovation

Community college faculty—especially those teaching in small colleges and in rural areas—have few opportunities to interact with peers, try out new ideas, or learn about new methods. Teaching is a demanding, full-time vocation. In 2002, RTS, with a grant from the Ford Foundation, set out to improve the situation by creating a multi-institutional forum for sharing, learning, and innovation. CraftNet became one of the first such communities of practice, or networks (see Resources for a list of members). Twelve community and technical colleges that either had strong arts and crafts programs or were in the process of building them were invited to form a pilot network to collectively use arts and crafts to serve students and to help build local economies. Member colleges set individual and collective goals. Patrick Henry Community College in Martinsville, Virginia, for example, was only at the starting gate when CraftNet formed, but, with advice and support from other members, now has a new facility, programs, and an exchange program with a CraftNet college from South Africa. Montana State University-Great Falls College of Technology has a new program to teach entrepreneurial skills to artisans. Mayland Community College in western North Carolina has a new apprenticeship and marketing program. Hazard Community and Technical College has opened its Kentucky School of Craft.

The Media Arts Alliance is another group of colleges—mostly urban—committed to improving technical programs

—continued

that support the large and growing but ill-defined jobs supporting the entertainment industry. Member colleges are working on defining curricula, skill, and education requirements and career paths; establishing industry partnerships and internships; and attracting nontraditional learners. Members are currently working jointly to create an international virtual world music or film festival that requires teamwork among students. The newest creative network is WineNet, a network of U.S. and Canadian colleges that have programs in viticulture and enology and, in most, operating vineyards and wineries.

This table was designed and built by a student in the fine woodworking program at Santa Fe Community College, New Mexico.

Photo courtesy of Santa Fe Community College.

Connecticut, Housatonic Community College's Museum of Art uses rotating theme-based exhibits to educate people about the area's past, social issues, and the arts themselves.

Independence Community College's William Inge Center for the Arts, located in a small Kansas town (9,000 population), became a regional hub for playwrights, performers, and directors. In addition to its well-known annual theater festival and regular plays, the college supports playwrights in residence, has a one-act competition, offers workshops, and has a rural arts education day. The college is now targeting high school arts programs. Despite the success, the arts programs struggle for resources, competing with training for industry and athletics (Hansen, 2004).

Greenfield Community College in rural Franklin County in western Massachusetts sits on the fringe of what is quickly becoming a major creative enterprise cluster. Creative Western Massachusetts has been a lifesaver for a region that had lost much of the manufacturing on which it depended so heavily for decades—metals around Springfield, plastics in the Berkshires, and furniture in the northern tier. Today, with support from foundations and the state, the region is building on its existing tourist attractions such as the Tanglewood and the Berkshire ski areas to reinvent itself as a center for creative arts. Although the region is home to many distinguished colleges and universities that offer fine arts, Greenfield Community College is finding a niche for itself as the pipeline for the creative subcultures in the region. The college has 930 students in its arts courses and 800 alumni living in its service area, which includes Northampton and Brattleboro, Vermont, both among the 100 top art cities in America (Villani, 2005). The local public media, along with the community college, are creating a humanities portal to allow people to learn what is available. The college is increasing its emphasis on music and intends to build a new performance center in Greenfield.

4. Recommendations

What can and should community colleges do to support the arts, culture, and the kinds of creative economies they imply? How do the arts and culture help students find employment, perform on the job, and move up career ladders? How can they overcome the conventional wisdom that art and business are polar opposites and that commercial success undermines art?

Community colleges can help by finding ways to integrate the arts and design into technical and commercial curricula and business concepts into arts and design programs so that students have a common language and understand the interdependencies. Colleges can also help by providing some of the business functions that handcrafters and digital designers dislike so that they can concentrate more on their core competencies—which most likely do not include marketing or accounting. European colleges may seem more effective at integrating art, industry, and design, and their governments are more supportive of creative industries, perhaps because they have a longer tradition in Europe.

Arts and design can

- enrich the colleges' learning environment in ways that improve the creative abilities and employability of students;

- enlarge the economic base of a community in areas not previously emphasized;

- attract marginalized populations into a learning environment in which they are comfortable and can succeed; and

- add to a community's quality of life and make it more attractive to talent and knowledge-based companies.

The following recommendations assume that the arts, design, and culture represent not just a measure of quality of life but also business opportunities, competitive niches, and local amenities.

1. Incorporate Art and Design in Technical and Commercial Programs

Art and design used to be part of vocational education and were called the manual and domestic arts. American manufacturing was, until approximately the 1930s, primarily a craft in which success depended largely on the novelty of the product (Scranton, 1997). Industrialized nations may have to return to their traditional niches in novelty and design and target markets where aesthetics, not price, is the decisive factor for consumers. The traditional manufacturing clusters that have continued to prosper in northern Italy, for example, are those that incorporate art and design in their products. This suggests that the workforce ought to have the skills needed to produce highly crafted or designer goods and creative services.

Adding the element of art and design to already overloaded technical and commercial curricula will be challenged by competing interests and similar demands from, for example, those exhorting colleges to increase emphasis on math and science, entrepreneurship, international skills, or the humanities. The tipping point may be the realization that colleges that teach creativity or use the arts to improve other workplace skills find that it (a) boosts interest in traditional programs that have had trouble attracting students and (b) improves core skills.

- The integration of the arts into the welding program at Bellingham Technical College in Washington increased welding skills and also attracted students.

- In Ireland, Galway-Mayo Institute of Technology's Furniture College requires design and manufacturing students to work as teams for 30 weeks on real industry projects.

2. Teach Business and Entrepreneurial Skills in Creative Occupation Programs

Historically, education institutions placed arts for artists under the liberal arts, as courses to give students a well-rounded, not occupationally grounded, education. Because the arts are not intended to prepare students for the workplace, they include little if any practical business or entrepreneurial education. Yet business skills are more important to the creative individual who is far more likely to have to manage a business than is the typical community college graduate.

The creative sector is dominated by independent artists, freelancers, and consultants and by microenterprises, and in no other economic sector is entrepreneurial skill more important. Even hair stylists are more likely to own their own shop, or chair, than be employed. In the industry classification "arts, entertainment, and recreation," 30% of those working are self-employed. Therefore, it should not be surprising that many community colleges are attempting to introduce more business education into their programs and to develop business support programs for students once they have left the college.

- Montana State University-Great Falls College of Technology has created a new associate degree program (TRACE) that focuses on creating entrepreneurial artists and designers who know how to write a business plan, manage cash flow, and market their goods.

- Haywood Community College in Clyde, North Carolina, has integrated a proven national entrepreneurship curriculum called REAL Enterprises into its crafts programs. The college also runs a summer boot camp to teach business skills to artisans.

3. Provide Business Services to Craft-Based Enterprises and Artistic Services to Mass Market Enterprises

Beginning in the early 1980s, community colleges assumed responsibilities for delivering real services to companies. Changes in company organization or technology, colleges discovered, required retraining and well-equipped labs, and centers at colleges could be used to induce companies to modernize. The advanced technology centers became the most popular mechanism for and the forerunner of the manufacturing extension partnership. That same model designed for small manufacturers can be applied to creative enterprises that need help with areas in which they lack expertise, which may include solving technical production problems, purchasing supplies, marketing, designing and supporting Web sites, raising capital, or simply finding partners. Technical programs working with manufacturers can link those that need help with design with local companies or student interns.

- Dundalk Institute of Technology in Ireland, in cooperation with a local university and Dream Ireland, Ltd., launched the Midas Project in June 2004 to support companies in film and video technology, animation, computer games, and digital design. As lead college, the institute will assist with research projects, skill development, and business assistance.

- Edmonds Community College in Washington and Haywood Community College in North Carolina are hosting Art Business Institute Workshops, which provide knowledge about product development, pricing, public relations, wholesaling, and accounting to artisans, gallery owners, and small business owners.

4. Find Innovative Ways To Attract and Support Nontraditional and Reentering Students

The arts and design are an underused entry or reentry gateway to education. Many of the programs in the arts, design, and creative occupations are overwhelmingly populated by nontraditional students—defined by age, educational background, socioeconomic status, or ethnicity. The handicrafts tend to draw older people, most of whom have been out of school for some time. Because it takes time to build a customer base, handicrafts appeal to people who have assets and are changing careers, who are looking for secondary incomes by turning their hobbies or interests into businesses, or who have few other choices.

Programs that target the entertainment industries draw younger students, many of whom have rejected schooling but are attracted back to programs that connect to their interests and environment. The digital creative and design industries attract a younger population of students that has both the computer skills and artistic talents, as well as more educated career changers from other technical fields. Each of these populations calls for a different marketing strategy and different support system. Older students and career changers may begin in continuing education and advance into degree programs. They need stronger peer support, flexible scheduling, and child care. Younger, more marginalized populations want programs concentrated heavily on their interests and on introducing basic skills. They will be attracted to programs that can connect quickly to their interests and artistic talents.

- Programs in the arts and crafts can be effective in attracting large numbers of nontraditional students. In the crafts programs at the College of Technology at Great Falls, Montana, for example, 62% of students have scholarships, 86% are older than 30, and 62% are from outlying rural areas.

- Through its music technology programs, Shoreline Community College north of Seattle attracts higher proportions of people of color and nontraditional students of all ages than does the college as a whole. They include ethnically diverse, young, or under-employed enrollees who may be seeking certificates or degrees or are just trying out some college courses. Three out of four students work part- or full-time, with an average income of less than $12,000.

- The Harlan campus of the Southeast Kentucky Community College, in one of America's most persistently poor areas, used its local artistic and cultural assets to help overcome poverty and substance abuse. With support from the Rockefeller Foundation, programs on digital photography

to preserve the region's history ("scanning bees"), storytelling and listening, and ceramics for public art were all used to raise skill levels, generate pride in place, and overcome social problems.

5. Partner With Arts and Cultural Organizations To Reach Out to the Community

Community colleges are accustomed to sitting at the table with economic development officials, employers, and chamber executives—but not with the arts community. Rarely will a community college official serve on an arts council board or vice versa. North Carolina is one such rarity, with a system president having served as past chairman of the North Carolina Arts Council. North Carolina has given the arts priority, and the state offices are a showroom for students' arts and crafts. North Carolina had a Visiting Artist Program in partnership with the North Carolina Arts Council from the 1970s until 1995, when lack of funds shut it down. It placed professional artists on community college campuses to practice their arts. Some of the artists stayed with the colleges and started new arts programs. A number of colleges partner with non-profit organizations to support and promote museums and performance and cultural centers that bring music, theater, and dance to the community at large.

- Bucks County Community College in Pennsylvania has operated an Artmobile since 1975 to bring art into the community and public schools. Now in a 48-foot trailer, the Artmobile stops throughout the county at libraries, community spaces, and schools, targeting its exhibits to its audience and providing audiences with printed materials.

- Mayland Community College in North Carolina, in partnership with HandMade in America, established a crafts, aquaponics, and organic gardening incubator and crafts gallery—all powered by methane released from a landfill.

6. Define Economic Opportunities, Skill Requirements, and Pathways for Successful Careers in the Arts and Design

Occupational and entrepreneurial opportunities in many of the creative enterprises are undercounted and underdocumented. The former National Skills Standards Board combined arts and entertainment with sectors like telecommunications, computer services, and information services—all of which received far greater attention. There is a need to document entry points and advancement opportunities for arts- and design-related careers to make the opportunities more transparent and available to high school and college counselors, workforce boards, and employment agencies, as South Africa has done through its Sector Skills Council. This type of work has untapped potential for attracting and retaining many nontraditional learners. Some agency or coalition of agencies, however, has to step up and take responsibility for

- defining occupations in terms of content, core skills, skills that provide the holder with advantages that lead to advancemant in the job queue, educational qualifications, and experience requirements;

- describing workplace context and special conditions that affect work schedules, responsibilities, physical demands, etc.;

- estimating projected demand both for employment and markets;

- mapping career paths in terms of alternative entry points, employment and entrepreneurial potential, skills and credentials needed for advancement or economic success, and sources of support; and

- establishing articulation agreements with secondary schools and baccalaureate programs.

A few places where the labor market demand for the creative industries is obvious have developed requirements for some fields:

- The Private Industry Council for Silicon Valley developed a labor market analysis for the digital media industry that described specific skills, core competencies, educational requirements, and "star qualities" for occupations in the cluster.

- Santa Monica Community College's Academy for Entertainment and Technology offers a "Middle College" summer program to enable high school students to build a portfolio that will help them qualify for its college programs.

7. Support Professional Development and Interinstitutional Learning

Professional development and opportunities to interact with peers and benchmark other programs are especially important for faculty in creative occupational programs, which are more varied and have fewer standards and benchmarks for best practices. Community college faculty carry heavy teaching loads that allow little time for curriculum development, innovation, and learning. Faculty exchanges, study tours, and networking produce innovative results. Resources ought to be set aside for professional development and collaborative activities, such as learning and innovations alliance.

- CraftNet, managed by RTS under a grant from the Ford Foundation, is an alliance of 13 colleges from the United States, United Kingdom, and South Africa working toward more effective and innovative ways to prepare and support arts- and crafts-based education programs and enterprise development.

- The Media Arts Alliance, also managed by RTS, is a similar alliance of 10 colleges from the United States, South Africa, and Germany developing innovative programs for jobs and companies that support the music, film, video, and digital entertainment industries. Colleges, for example, are working toward a virtual international music festival that will travel among states and countries and operate in different environments and cultures.

8. Designate Specific Colleges as Lead Institutions, or "Cluster Hubs," for Arts and Arts-Based Industries

In many states and nations that have adopted clusters as organizing frameworks for economic development, community colleges are considering models to fit those frameworks. Many have already developed a critical mass of expertise and have become de facto "cluster hubs" by responding to the specialized needs of regional industry concentrations. Creative enterprise economies, however, are rarely considered for cluster hubs in the United States.

Specialized colleges that do not offer a baccalaureate for arts, crafts, and design are more common in other industrialized countries where the crafts and design have been held in greater esteem. In the United States, such colleges—especially if they also included the digital arts—could be a major creative engine for regional economies.

- The mission of Santa Monica Community College's Academy for Entertainment and Technology is to prepare students to become flexible professionals in the fast-changing media fields. Because the school is near the heart of Southern California's entertainment cluster, the program has an active industry advisory board, and students can intern with industry partners.

- The Glamorgan Centre for Arts and Design Technology, which is part of Coleg Morgannwg in Wales, has a world-class animation program. Students begin by learning learn handcrafts and then move into the digital skills. Students each year compete for "Glammies," and graduates are prime candidates for Disney, BBC, and other major media companies.

- The Los Angeles campus of the Fashion Institute of Design and Merchandising is in the heart of the city's international craft and media industries and prepares students in fashion, visual arts, graphic design, interior design, and entertainment. The 30-year-old, 5,000-student college awards associate in arts degrees and advanced study programs in 14 industry majors. With close ties to industry, it maintains an alumni network of 30,000 to help advise and place students.

9. Establish Internship Programs With Artisans and Industry

Despite the abundance of evidence of the value of experiential learning, most U.S. programs have little, if any, work-based learning requirements. The arts, crafts, and design lend themselves particularly well to apprenticing, learning from masters, and learning from one another. Only so much can be learned from textbooks; therefore, the curricula for creative occupations ought to include a significant number of internship or apprenticeship credits. Existing federally funded apprenticeship programs, however, do not yet recognize these fields. In addition, internships that place artists and designers in manufacturing and commercial firms might demonstrate to the companies the value of the arts and design and give students a chance to learn about the commercial parts of their business. Businesses, in turn, can learn from the creative impulses of the artists and designers.

- The Massachusetts Cultural Council provides grants of up to $6,000 for a traditional arts apprenticeship program in which individuals work with master artists and craftspeople.

- HandMade in America is jointly establishing an apprenticeship program for a Studio Technician with Haywood Community College in North Carolina that alternates classroom education and working with an artisan–mentor.

10. Design Creativity Benchmarks for Community Colleges

Community colleges need to establish benchmarks to assess their effectiveness in using and cultivating the arts and culture to support the creative needs of their economies; such standards have been recommended for universities. Similar standards would help colleges to measure their own progress over time and, if done for a system, know where they might want to consider change. Sample benchmarks are as follows.

- Percentage of total resources allocated to arts and design.

- Number of arts of design programs available.

- Percentage of hours in arts or design in technical and commercial curricula.

- External or community programs in arts sponsored by the college annually.

- Percentage of graduates completing programs for creative occupations.

- Number of nontraditional students enrolled in creative programs and retention rates.

- Release time and resources for faculty learning and development.

- Internships and employment relationships with creative enterprises.

Photo courtesy of Independence Community College, William Inge Theatre Festival.

Students perform *Inherit the Wind* at Independence Community College, Kansas. The college's William Inge Center for the Arts has become a regional hub for playwrights, performers, and directors.

5. On Becoming a Cool Community College

Predicting that creative expression will be one of the larger sources of growth and advantage in the future does not take special insight. In a global economy, industrialized nations with high costs will have to find new advantages. Although industries that use advanced technologies rely on research and development and find niche products that are not easily imported are the most obvious targets, cultural tourism, creative services, and crafted products will also become significant sources of growth, especially in smaller cities and rural areas (Villani, 2005).

How can a community college orient its place in the community as the most accessible source of learning and knowledge about this new and less familiar target of economic opportunity for their students and regions? The more familiar and traditional role of the community college in the economy has been as a source of technical skills and information. Community colleges have paid far less attention to the creative and artistic aspects of work, forms of growth, or types of students. Will community colleges be able and willing to adapt to the needs of companies that depend on originality and new forms of expression? What will be the hallmarks of the community colleges and systems that do try to integrate creativity and culture more deeply into their programs and institutions? The colleges and college systems that do may take on some of the following characteristics.

- Community college systems will understand the roles that creative sectors can play in their regions and the potential value of art and design as competitive advantages in other sectors and integrate that knowledge into plans and priorities.

- Students in technical and commercial programs will be encouraged—and, in some

The old mill house is on the main campus of Haywood Community College, located in western North Carolina's scenic Blue Ridge Mountains.

Photo by Debra Davis, courtesy of Haywood Community College.

programs, required—to take applied arts or design courses. The arts will also be incorporated into some process courses to cultivate creativity and enhance communications skills, which will increase employability and productivity.

- Programs intended to develop a student's talents and knowledge in career fields based on arts and design will be offered in both applied arts and applied sciences tracks, with options for transfer in both as continuing education.

- Students who wish to apply their creative talents to earn a living will be encouraged and supported with programs of study that include not only studio techniques but also business and entrepreneurial competencies, marketing and networking skills, and opportunities to apprentice with masters.

- The arts and design will attract new and nontraditional learners into college courses that match their recreational interests and reward their untapped talents with the expectation that early successes will encourage them to continue along career pathways and perhaps into degree programs.

- Community colleges will work hand in hand with local arts councils, design centers, and economic development agencies to bring cultural and recreational attractions to the community.

Looking to industries that produce arts and crafts is still a risky path to take in economic development if viewed in isolation, but if matched with parallel investments in compatible knowledge-intensive industries that appreciate the arts and culture and that thrive on design, it may be the most promising path. The community colleges that choose a path toward fostering a creative economy give students these opportunities and support them as they develop their skills. Those that integrate the arts and design most effectively into their programs, pedagogies, and institutional culture are likely to have a positive influence on the future of their students and communities.

Galway-Mayo Institute of Technology's new campus façade at night.

Photo courtesy of GMIT.

References

Baldacci, J. E. (2004, April 9). Address at Bates College, Lewiston-Auburn, Maine.

Baldacci, J. E. (2005). *An order to advance Maine's creative economy.* Available from www.maine. gov/gov/baldacci/news

Barboza, D. (2004, December 24). In roaring China, sweaters are west of sock city. *New York Times,* p. A-1.

Bettoli, M., & Micelli, S. (2005). *The strategic role of design for the competitiveness of Italian Industrial Systems,* Unpublished paper, Venice International University, Venice, Italy.

Cortright, J., & Mayer, H. (2002). *Signs of life: The growth of biotechnology centers in the U.S.* Washington, DC: The Brookings Institution.

Cox, J. B. (2005, February 17). Art.com raising $30 million. *Raleigh News & Observer,* p. D-1.

Coy, M. (2004, November 4–5). *Colleges that do it in style: Examples from around the world.* Plenary session, conference on Community Colleges in Creative Economies, Asheville, NC. Available from www.rtsinc.org/ asheville/pdf/Coy.pdf

Davis, K. (2004, July 7). Asheville's cool factor is translating into new jobs. *Asheville Citizen-Times.*

Federal Reserve Bank of Atlanta. (2005). Challenges loom large for southeastern textile producers and cotton growers. *EconSouth, 7*(2).

Fields, J. (2003). *The craft heritage trails of western North Carolina* (3rd ed.). Asheville, NC: HandMade in America.

Florida, R. (2002). *The rise of the creative class.* New York: Basic Books.

Hansen, J. (2004, November 4–5). *College support for creative environment: Independence Community College William Inge Center for the Arts.* Presentation at the conference on Community Colleges in Creative Economies, Asheville, NC. Available from www.rtsinc. org/asheville/pdf/Hansen.pdf

Hecker, D. (2004, February). Occupational employment projections to 2012. *Monthly Labor Review.*

Kavanagh, R. (2004, November 4–5). *Creative individuals: Integrating art and design into technical and commercial curricula.* Workshop at the conference on Community Colleges in Creative Economies, Asheville, NC.

Lancaster, H. M. (2004, November 4–5). "*Making it new" in community colleges.* Opening remarks at the conference on Community Colleges in Creative Economies, Asheville, NC. Available from www.rtsinc.org/ asheville/pdf/Lancaster.pdf

McCarthy, K. F., Ondaatje, E. H., Zakaras, L., & Brooks, A. (2004). *Gifts of the muse: Reframing the debate about the benefits of the arts*. Santa Monica: RAND Corporation. Available from www.rand.org/pubs/monographs/2005/RAND_MG218.pdf

New England Council. (2000, June). *The creative economy initiative: The role of the arts and culture in New England's economic competitiveness*. Available from www.nefa.org/pubs

New England Council. (2001, June). *The creative economy initiative: A blueprint for investment in New England's creative economy*. Available from www.nefa.org/pubs

Nussbaum, B. (2005, July 4). Annual design awards. *Business Week*, p. 62.

Paine, N. (2004, November 4–5). *Putting creativity into the workforce*. Address at the conference on Community Colleges in Creative Economies, Asheville, NC. Available from www.rtsinc.org/asheville/pdf/Paine.pdf

Pink, D. H. (2005, February). Revenge of the right brain. *WIRED*.

Pumphrey, G. (2004, November 4–5). *Creativity and steel: Can a college weld together an economic impact?* Presentation at the conference on Community Colleges in Creative Economies, Asheville, NC. Available from www.rtsinc.org/asheville/pdf/Pumphrey.pdf

Read, H. (1953). *Art in industry*. Bloomington: Indiana University Press.

Rose, M. (2004). *The mind at work: Valuing the intelligence of the American worker*. New York: Viking Press.

Rosenfeld, S. (2001). Rural community colleges: Creating institutional hybrids for the New Economy. *Rural America, 16*(2), 2–8.

Rosenfeld, S. (2004a, Summer). Crafting a new rural development strategy. *Economic Development America,* 11–13. Available from www.eda.gov

Rosenfeld, S. (2004b). Design as competitive advantage: The creative enterprise cluster in the western United States. *European Planning Studies, 12*(12), pp. 891–904

Scranton, P. (1997). *Endless novelty: Specialty production and American industrialization, 1865–1925*. Princeton, NJ: Princeton University Press.

Tibbetts, M. (2004, November 4–5). *The creative industries cluster initiative in Scotland*. Presentation at the conference on Community Colleges in Creative Economies, Asheville, NC. Available from www.rtsinc.org/asheville/pdf/Tibbetts.pdf

VanAusdle, S. L. (2004, November 4–5). *Enhancing Rural Prosperity via Wine, Food, and Art*. Presentation at the conference on Community Colleges in Creative Economies, Asheville, NC. Available from www.rtsinc.org/asheville/pdf/VanAusdle.pdf

Villani, J. (2005). *The 100 best art towns in America: A guide to galleries, museums, festivals, lodging and dining* (4th ed.). Santa Fe: John Muir Publications.

West German Chamber of Handicrafts Association. (1989). *The handicrafts trade in North Rhine Westphalia*. Dusseldorf: Ministry of Industry, Small- and Medium-Sized Business and Technology of North Rhine.

Williams, B. (2004, November 4–5). *Creatively Munro*. Presentation at the conference on Community Colleges in Creative Economies, Asheville, NC. Available from www.rtsinc.org/asheville/pdf/Williams.pdf

Resources

Benchmark Practice Web Links

College of the Redwoods Fine Furniture
Program, CA
www.crfinefurniture.com

CraftNet, NC
www.rtsinc.org/craftnet/index.html

CreateSA, South Africa
www.createsa.org.za

Creative Clusters, United Kingdom
www.creativeclusters.com

Creative Economy Council, MA
www.creative-economy.org

EnergyXchange, NC
www.energyxchange.org

Finlandia University School of Art and Design, MI
www.finlandia.edu/flashpage.html

Galway-Mayo Institute of Technology Furniture
College, Ireland
www.gmit.ie/prospective_students/prospectus
2005/campus/letterfrack

Greenfield Community College, MA
www.gcc.mass.edu

HandMade in America, NC
www.handmadeinamerica.org

Independence Community College William Inge
Center for the Arts, KS
www.ingefestival.org

Montana State University-Great Falls College
of Technology
www.msugf.edu

Montana Creative Enterprise Cluster
www.rtsinc.org/whatsnew.html

New Brunswick College of Craft and Design,
Canada
www.nbccd.nb.ca

New Media Alliance, NC
www.rtsinc.org

Penland School of Crafts, NC
www.penland.org

Regional Technology Strategies, NC
(Asheville conference)
www.rtsinc.org/Asheville

Scottish Enterprise Creative Industries Cluster
www.scottish-enterprise.com

Walla Walla Community College Institute for
Enology and Viticulture, WA
www.wwcc.edu/programs/proftech/wine

Creative Economy Learning Networks

CraftNet

Esayidi FET College, Gamalakhe Campus, Port Shepstone, South Africa

Glamorgan Centre for Art and Design Technology, Coleg Morgannwg, Pontypridd, Wales

Haywood Community College, Clyde, NC

Hazard Community and Technical College, KY

Hocking College, Nelsonville, OH

Mayland Community College, Spruce Pine, NC

Mnambithi FET College, Ladysmith, South Africa

Montana State University-Great Falls College of Technology

Patrick Henry Community College, Martinsville, VA

Plymouth College of Art and Design, United Kingdom

Santa Fe Community College, NM

Southeast Kentucky Community and Technical College, Cumberland

Southern West Virginia Community and Technical College, Mt. Gay

Media Arts Alliance

Coleg Morgannwg, Pontypridd, Wales

Durban Institute of Technology, South Africa

Guilford Technical Community College, Jamestown, NC

Houston Community College System-Northwest College, TX

Howard Community College, Columbia, MD

Mission College, Santa Clara, CA

Shoreline Community College, Seattle, WA

Siemens Professional Education, Berlin, Germany

South Louisiana Community College, New Iberia

Valencia Community College, Orlando, FL

WineNet

Chemeketa Community College, Salem, OR

Davidson County Community College, Lexington, NC

Grayson County College, Denison, TX

Niagara College Glendale Campus, Niagara-on-the-Lake, Ontario, Canada

Okanagan University College, British Columbia, Canada

Otago Polytechnic, Cromwell, New Zealand

Santa Rosa Junior College, CA

Shawnee Community College, Ullin, IL

Surry Community College Foundation, Dobson, NC

Walla Walla Community College, WA

About the Author

Stuart Rosenfeld is founder and president of Regional Technology Strategies, Inc., a nonprofit organization located in Carrboro, North Carolina, that is dedicated to researching, designing, implementing, and assessing regional development strategies. He has more than 30 years of experience in policy analysis, formulation, and evaluation, with an emphasis on rural development, education and training, technology diffusion, and clusters and networks. Rosenfeld founded and directs the activities of the Trans-Atlantic Technology and Training Alliance, an international consortium of community and technical colleges in the United States, Europe, and South Africa.

Rosenfeld previously served as deputy director of the Southern Growth Policies Board, where he founded and directed the Southern Technology Council. Prior to joining Southern Growth, he was a senior associate at the National Institute of Education, where he co-authored a congressionally mandated assessment of vocational education. Previously he directed a private elementary school in Vermont and worked for 10 years for General Electric Company in manufacturing and operations research.

Rosenfeld has published numerous books and articles, including three through Community College Press: *New Technologies and New Skills: Two-Year Colleges at the Vanguard of Modernization; Advancing Opportunity in Advanced Manufacturing: The Potential for Predominantly Minority Two-Year Colleges;* and *learning.now: Skills for an Information Economy.*

Rosenfeld graduated cum laude in chemical engineering from the University of Wisconsin-Madison and earned his doctorate in education policy at Harvard University, where he served on the editorial board of the *Harvard Educational Review.* He is a senior policy fellow for the Southern Growth Policies Board and a senior research associate with the Community College Research Center at Teachers College. In 2004 he was honored with a Lifetime Achievement award by The Competitiveness Institute in Barcelona.

Index

small businesses. *See also* business of arts and design;
craft-based services; creative enterprises
business and entrepreneurial skills for, 34
as creative enterprises, 12
South Africa
CraftNet and, 31
Sector Skills Council, 37
Technikons and Further Education and Training
colleges, 28
Southeast Kentucky Community and Technical
College, Harlan County, 22, 36
Southern Growth Policies board, v
students. *See also* nontraditional learners with
creative talent
learning outcomes and labor market value, 6
nontraditional and reentering, attracting and
supporting, 35–36
Suomi College, Hancock, MI, International School
of Art and Design at, 20

Taos, NM, creative enterprises cluster of, 14–15
Taos Arts Association, 15
Taos Society of Artists, 14–15
Technikons, South Africa, 28
technology, art, and, 22
textile manufacturing, in China *versus* U.S., 2–3
Tilden Arts Center, Cape Cod Community College,
MA, 31

total education philosophy, v
TRACE (Transforming Regional Artisans into
Creative Enterprises), 29, 34
Trans-Atlantic Technology and Training Alliance
(TA^3), vii–viii

underserved populations, arts, design programs
and, 25–26
University of North Carolina Office of Economic
and Business Development, vii

Virginia, Appalachian Regional Commission
economic development grants in, 6
Visiting Artist Program, NC, vi, 36
Vorarlberg, Austria, textile manufacturing in, 15

Walla Walla Community College, WA, 30–31
Wallace State Community College, AL, 21
(The) Walt Disney Company, 22
Whole Foods Market, 26
Wilkes Community College, NC, 1
WineNet, 32
WIRED, 22
WoodFair, College of the Redwoods, CA, 27
workers, imaginative, 12–13. *See also* business skills
in creative occupation programs